God Created the Universe in Five Days

By Curtis R. Crim

ISBN: 978-0-9888255-5-0

Printed in the United States of America

First Printing

In loving memory of my beautiful girl Squeaky

TABLE OF CONTENTS

Preface

Every year as I work my organic farm, my mind wanders off into bizarre places. I sometimes find myself laughing, and try to devise a mnemonic to remember what made me laugh until I can get to my computer to write it down. Many of the jokes are lost, and I find that I can only remember about three new jokes at a time until I get to commit them to a file.

I didn't think up as many jokes this year as I have the last two, but several of the jokes I wrote this year are some of my favorites of all time.

Some of my jokes are really just random weirdness, and not really funny at all, and others make me laugh out loud every time I read them. I also categorize some of them as "dirty jokes". This is a bit misleading, because almost *every* joke I make up is "dirty" in some way.

Not every person will be equally entertained by my humor, but I hope that you find a few jokes amusing enough to pass on to friends, coworkers, and family members. Also, I strongly recommend that you be *fucked up* when you read this book!

Enjoy!
Curtis

Chapter 1: One-Liners

At least a human, you don't have to pluck!

Did you know that you can buy Evil off of the dollar menu?

I only talk to myself when I am present.

There is no "reason" in "treason".

Yes waiter, I'd like a little cunt stew.

I make soup, thyme and thyme again.

I taught myself to poop on newspaper.

Satan took a crap; he named it George.

Blaming the victim is American tradition.

If someone is killed by God, is it considered murder?

Are we not all multi-cellular orgasms, my love?

When you have been belted by a Dad hand, you have been dealt a BAD hand!

As Freud once said, "There always is more than one entrance into someone's ass."

Well if my dick IS deaf and blind, then why the fuck is *it* driving?

I never get to *touch* pussies, but I do get to *click* on them...

I have no family, but *they* **have** *me*!

Tell me this, why do Gorge W. Bush's fist *and arm* smell like Obama's asshole?

For a redneck, today is "sonny partly rowdy."

One of my sisters is an only child.

Out here on the farm, the *hen* is quicker than the eye!

I always find sex awesome, because I am having it with *myself*!

Slavery is just a way of getting to know foreign people.

The shit I make will far outlive the shit I am!

Sanity is a terrible thing to inflict on anyone...

Even on Wikipedia, a heterosexual woman is defined as a "Mythological creature."

I fell down and broke my hernia...

Do they have psychotherapy for chickens?

On my organic farm, I grow space and thyme...

That wood is knot Wright.

I sometimes think that strangers are the only friends I have.

I live in a universe with a population of one.

I never get to have *cunt-act* with females.

Even gay men get more pussy than I do!

Colon cancer is such a bunch of crap!

As far as human contact goes, for me, cats are *more* than enough!

I have a psychic connection with my penis...

Cathaholics drink *way* too much religion!

I am always the *last* to know anything about myself!

They say that "Time kills", so I call a clock a "nec-chronometer".

Ever heard about a "cross-world" puzzle?

Am I a loser or a wiener?

Actually, for a Chinese hooker, she was pretty conservative!

I am a jack-off all trades.

He's not the sort of cat who *doesn't* like to vomit...

All religion is blasphemy.

I have been celibate for sex years.

Is there such a thing as "*Gay*coupage"?

Is there *really* a team called the "Green gay-packers"?

I think about hot chicks in my in*vag*ination.

WMD = with my desire

Never make your bed and eat it too.

Current day medical science is shit, and it always has been!

An apple a day keeps the doctor away and a clove of raw garlic a day will keep away pretty much everyone else!

If it's a good day to die, then it's a good butt to *buy*!

He looks so short that he can't help but to be angry.

I am not sure if I'll get laid tonight. I'll check my whoreoscope.

Taking a dead dog for a walk is *such* a DRAG!

My parents were violently into peace.

Mass manufactured foods are total carbage!

I consider myself an "ad-liberal".

I am celibate as FUCK!

Women look really good on paper...

Like the Teamsters, are the Lobsters a union?

There was this dude whose brow bone was so low that it was part of his pelvis!

They love cars on Road Island.

I don't even own a vice and yet it is also all I have...

Everything else about her is pretty, but her nose is a real slap in the face!

My father was brilliant, but he was so lazy that he was professionally incapacitated!

For a young teenage girl, tits are a nice new development.

My cat is like Obama; he is black and white.

My aunt's only job right now is to die, so she sleeps a lot for practice.

Sometimes it takes a village idiot to raze a village.

Mexican chickens are known as "Chickanos".

You can't squeeze blood from a rock, or moral good from a Bush!

I was tired of being told what to do before being born...

I felt guilty for making love to a married woman, but it wasn't so bad because she was *my* wife.

What kind of a cult is a difficult?

A cougar on cocaine can be a serious problem!

Ever hear of a legless, toothless prison bitch named "lucky"?

I am proud of my child who is an insidious creature with no soul...

I was always "struggling to find myself" until I got a GPS.

Luck be a labia night!

My vagina aches every time I look at a beautiful woman.

I'll bet that George W. Bush has his hands in Obama Care up to his elbows!

If you haven't gone too far, then you have not gone far enough!

I AM a redneck; I'm just not a MAIN STREAM redneck!

I have tried to introduce my dick to a woman before, but it has never tried to introduce me to one...

Stores have gone down hill since they made laws against stocking...

Mommy and Daddy loves day chillin'.

It is hard to lose weight if your body doesn't have enough dietoms.

Two women can experience "un-cunt-ditional" love.

It's not that men are necrophiliacs some times per se, but occasionally whomever you are fucking *dies in the act*!

I know a "good old egg" who said that he makes himself an omelet every night...

Don't get stung; just let it bee honey.

I can make a woman reject me using pure mental energy!

They have Worcestershire sauce, but not one based on peace.

Have you ever heard of a pandering bear?

Can you rape a woman *by accident*?

Bill had Monica squealing like Ned Beatty!

Most people are too poor to *not* be hated by billionaires!

Billionaires don't consider the rest of us real people.

Are "period music" and "Ragtime" the same?

It's not that my wife has a reason to yell at me; she just can't think of a reason *not* to!

The ambitious executioner worked hard to get a head!

On a farm, there is never enough time, and yet I grow bunches of it!

A woman is of no use if she is not willing to sometimes be whoreazontal.

It is difficult to be a virgin and a pervert at the same time, but somehow when I was a teenager, I managed it!

I am always nervous to hit on a woman; when it comes to sex, I am a total pussy!

Do women walk around in *broad* daylight?

"There's no accounting for a person's taste." said the cannibal.

I sure have met a lot of women whose name was, "Not".

Have you ever seen a fly run into a wok?

They say that love hurts, well, I say that squash hurts!

I have heard that imitation is the highest form of flattery, and I have always *loved* to flatter females!

Well, I might aim to misbehave, but I still want *it* to behave!

Well, I was a professional kazooist for 25 years...

I was so horney that I planted a pussy willow.

I used to think that artificial colors and flavors were necessary digestive enzymes!

I dream of pussy.

This kitty was getting ready to tear me up, but she lacked ingredients and decided to start from scratch.

I hate my asshole; it's FULL OF SHIT!

It's okay gals; you don't have to go to college to get raped...

How can I be surrounded by cats and never get any pussy?

Have you ever asked a woman if you can have a date with her after she had died?

Have you heard of the Department of Just Ass?

Cute little girls are only hot for a few years, but you can be a dirty old man at *any age*!

Unless a woman is a contortionist, it seems hard to get her to *cough* up a little pussy.

I am a *firm* believer in how sexy women are.

Well, it wasn't in my home cuntry, but I did have some pussy for a few days a *broad*.

Everyone I know has Been Laden, and I haven't!

Around my property, I put up "No Stresspassing" signs.

Well, if cat hair gets you high, then I sure as *fuck* am stoned on it!

If you are upset about what is happening to dolphins, then you have your priorities in terms of world affairs seriously out of order!

Now there is one zucchini I wood like to taste!

They say that it takes a village to raise a child, but a cat you can raise alone.

My planets make it so that I can't get laid; I have really bad *ass*-trology!

Why are there always misspellings in the way rednecks pronounce words?

Women have only *one* criterion for a boyfriend: that he is not *ME*!

Well, if I'm ever gang-banged in prison, I want to look my best!

Of vice and men…

I was Jewed up and spat out!

As long as she can breathe through her nose,
everything will probably be okay...

Even the word "slave" is not so bad in the RIGHT
CONTEXT!

As long as you are being *lied* to, you don't *need* any
rights!

Unfortunately for me, I am allergic to
antihistamines.

Nature *always* does its worst!

How long do you have to know a woman before it
is okay to rape her?

That donkey has a nice ass...

I'm no alcoholic; I spend some time NOT drunk
every day!

I just heard more thunder, so I'm expectin' more
participation!

I drink a lot of alcohol so that my *genius* doesn't get
out of control...

To get the tenderest human meat, keep a kid in bed
its whole life like veal, until you are ready to eat it.

I have heard of a play date; have you ever heard of
play date *rape*?

Well, if ignorance IS bliss, then there are a fucking LOT of *blissful* people in Iowa!

For me, being conventional was never an option.

Why do you think that more resolutions are made on New Year's Day than the NIGHT BEFORE?!

I have managed to produce everything I have marijuanted.

My cat is happy, or my hat is crappy; I am good either way.

I can create a universe but I can't exist in one.

I don't understand why so many women want to look hot but NEVER have sex with a man!

All I want for breakfast is my two front teeth!

She was more warm, but less hot.

Out on the farm, we use fur-mentation.

I brew a beet wine. I can "beet you up"!

Hell hath no fury like a woman.

Chapter 2: Short Jokes

This chapter is *not* about short people. It contains jokes that are not very long.

So you are going to *force* me to go to a seafood restaurant? That is so shellfish!

I am not objecting to the quality of the food. I just didn't think that there was enough *meat* to call it Emile.

I hate daylight savings time; after all, you can reset a clock, but you can't reset a cat!

When I ask a woman out, she *always* says, "No." For some reason, women always want to "no" me, but never want to "know" me!

Have you ever heard that in the Holy Bible it is said that the universe was created in seven days? Well, more specifically that God took *six* days to create everything, and then rested on the seventh day? *Actually* it was closer to five days, and she was "resting" the w*hole* time!

Well, I am 50 now, and it sucks in some ways. For one thing, most women my age are not interested in sex. And it's been like that my *entire* life!

As boys, we are told to grow into big men and kick ass. Jeffery Dahmer thought that they said, "Cook ass".

Every day at 4 in the morning, some cock wakes me up. How many women have the same experience?

The instructions said, "Serve on a bed of steamed rice." Now, assuming that I have company, how am I going to get a "bed" of rice that big?

I have sometimes heard about how stupid it is to put water in bottles, yet people have been putting bottles in water for centuries, and no one ever complained about that!

Dude: "It must suck to be you!"
Me: "Yes, and now it sucks just a little bit more because of you; thanks motherfucker!"

The advantage of being flora-sexual is that plants never object; they can't even say "Baaaa!" in an angry manner. I'm flora-sexual, but I have considered dating a woman who is either catatonic, or in a coma.

Being married was really awesome; my wife and I had sex every day. Sometimes, we even did it with each other!

Women who are heterosexuals are TOTALLY GAY! The only women I truly trust are *lesbians*.

I don't have paranoia; I have *Mara*noia. There's a difference.

I am NOT saying that men are naturally monogamous; I am saying that it is natural for a man to be monogamous with a *hole lot* of women at the same time.

I sometimes stutter when I *s*talk to myself; it's as though being around myself makes me nervous.

Maybe the Christians are not crazy. Maybe Christ *will* come again! Who do you think made him cum the first time?

Q: Do you have a Christmas stocking?
A: Yes, I have a couple of people who I plan to stalk for Christmas!

Don't let them teasing you about being fat bother you; you're bigger than that!

Not only did my mother die in child birth, but so did most of my family, and half of the hospital staff!

My cock could make my life so much better, but it doesn't. It goes out and gets laid regularly, but I haven't had sex in *years*!

"That dude's a dick!"
"I know. I am the one who addickted him!"

I have cousins whose wives have gone into menopause. I am now 50, and I have *never* even gotten a woman to pause!

Q: What kind of a tree is a cuntry?
A: It is a Pussy willow.

Woman: "Maybe we got off on the wrong foot."
Man: "I have not had a foot to get off on in years!"

I squeezed out two essays in two weeks, and my little hen squeezed out two eggs in a single morning, and *SHE* didn't even go to college!

Woman: "My husband was a wife beater."
Friend: "That's strange; he didn't strike me that way."

I was fucked by the Holy Spirit. I am now on *emission* from God!

It rained hard; I drank hard. The next morning, my flowers were all hung-over.

Woman at bar: "This is kind of lame. Want to get out of here?"
Me: "Okay. I'll leave, and it will improve."

Q: Why do cops use police dogs?
A: Because dogs work for food, and they are *way* smarter than cops!

The root of all evil is God. If you don't agree, then you simply are not paying attention to theological politics!

I don't hold it against you that you were born a woman in this lifetime. I hole in INSIDE YOU.

Life is so fucking weird! It might be real, but it's the *WRONG* REEL!

I am *really* into non-violence, but I don't always practice it *myself*!

I am the spiritual leader of a one-man commune...

Why is it that the early worm doesn't get the bird? It is like pre-mature ejaculation?

Did you know that binding the hands of most women actually makes their pussies wetter? Some men will tie a woman up purely for the purpose of getting improved lubrication.

Every girlfriend I ever had is now dead. In retrospect, I think I would have had a much better time if I had been a necrophiliac!

Have you ever taken a shit so beautiful that you thought, "I can't *believe* that this came out of me!"? Well, that's how I feel about this book. Strange that *my own* humor amuses me so much!

He would always talk about her?
No, he would always *stalk* about her.

You can take the presidency out of George W. Bush, but you can **NEVER** take George W. Bush out of the presidency!

I am not old; I just haven't managed to die yet!
Well, keep trying motherfucker!

Because I live in the middle of nowhere; I am automatically entitled to be eccentric.

I have 34 hens, but only got 9 eggs today. I suspect fowl play.

Why is it that some chicks can be "Jersey Whore" crazy, without even being drunk?! My wife was like that ALL OF THE FUCKING TIME!

Have you ever heard that someone can become a "functional psychotic"? You can also become a functional "alco-psychotic".

Chapter 3: Dirty Jokes

Ever wipe your butt then smear it on your chest?

They say that shit washes off a lot more easily than blood. However, gay men pretty much have to deal with both!

Q: Who can shit out blood and guts even though they don't eat meat?
A: A gay vegetarian!

You can lead a nose to asshole, but you can't make it stink...

Does the five second rule apply when something falls *directly into shit*?

I shove my cock in my girlfriend's asshole; I have her convinced that it is the best form of contraception.

I hate to not have my dick in one of my girlfriend's holes at all times, but as a gentleman, I am willing to let her blow me while she shits and pisses.

My aunt is so senile that she now "walks" herself. Fortunately, my mother follows her with a baggy and a scooper.

Riddle: A box without hinges, key or lid, yet inside golden showers are hid.

Sometimes I get some pussy discharge in my mouth when I kiss my cat on her cunt.

If you are performing cunnilingus on a cat, what is it called? It is like, "Pussy Squared"?

I tried to fuck that hole, but there was a crawdad in there!

I can't justify it. My nose was cold, and your butt is warm.

Do you ever butter your daughter's anus? For taste or lubrication?

Child molestation is not free; the places that will molest your child usually charge for their *service*.

What if a woman were to eat her aborted fetus, and go, "Oh my God this is delicious! I can't believe this came out of my PUSSY!"

My father was a teacher, and touched a lot of lives. My mother also touched a lot of people, but in an *entirely* different way! ;)

If you *do* need to take an enema 3 times a day, you have a strong libido, and you happen to be gay, then an enema bag with a dick-shaped delivery end becomes a reasonable solution!

I was a breach birth just so I could take more time *fucking my mother* on the way out!

By the end of his life, my father had mastered an *unassisted* self-crapping method.

Do you ever have to spit, and you don't want to waste it, so you rub it on your asshole?

When gay's have a party, they always create a *collective hole.*

"It's nice to meet you; I am going to cum in your vagina."

I have heard of fucking a cow, but it takes real balls to fuck a bull!

Sixty-nine buttholes of queer on my balls...

What my cock lacks in stature, it makes up for in enthusiasm!

Sometimes people just have that "child fucky" sort of vibe.

If I were to ever lose my right arm, I would want them to give me a prosthetic that was DESIGNED FOR JACKING OFF!!!

Vet: Your dog obviously loves me.
Me: Yep, but you DID rub his cock and balls!

Why do they put netting on the inside of men's swimming trunks? Is that so it will catch it if you crap out a turd?

It's not that child molesters use candy to lure in kids, so much that it is a matter of kids learning to whore themselves for candy before they learn to do it for drugs!

What do they call it when you are eating a woman's pussy while she is being fucked in the ass?

One time, I had an orgasm, shit, puked, pissed, astral-projected, and went insane all at once!

My cats tend to tear up my rubber...

How long should you date a person's pet before you *fuck* it?

It's not like I am asking you for a quart of blood, and if I were, I would at least have the courtesy to do it at an *appropriate time of the month*!

I hear that they now have prosthetic ass-ginas!

It's hard to say a "safe-word" with a giant cock stuffed down your throat!

So this bestialist hillbilly gets *disowned* by his family for fucking MALE animals!

Have you ever woken up and your fingers smelled like your butt? How about someone else's?

Do you like pork? To me, it depends on whether it is on my plate or in my ass!

It is hard for some of us to believe, but somewhere out there, there is some guy who is looking *forward* to going home and having sex with a ***goat***!

No guy who isn't willing to use his ASS on the way up is going anywhere. I always envisioned using my ass on my way going down...

Do you want to know why men like to have a conversation with your boobs? It is because it is a lot easier than having a conversation with your butt!

I could SHIT myself right now and still feel good about myself. I am that drunk! I am a God! If you try to attack me, at least I will still have *shit* to throw at you!

Chapter 4: Sex Jokes

I see there's a dent in yer pussy. I can bang that right out fur you!

How many times has a man *not* gotten laid because he let his brain take over instead of his dick?

Throwing short people into the mix is a low blow.

Maybe I *could* fuck a goat, but I just never met the right one...

Going without pussy is a long dry dong spell...

Have you ever heard of making "ends meat"? Well, ends don't meet, they mate!

Have you ever dated a necrophiliac? It's so annoying because they always want you to die before they fuck you!

My last girlfriend has been dead for over 25 years. Even a necrophiliac would have problems with that!

We can see from history that the Romans totally dominated the Greeks.
From what I heard, the Greeks had a pretty good time!

Does a lesbian ever want to strap one on and fuck a goat?

Well, if you are "getting it on", you might as well get it off!

Have you ever noticed that there are women who will make you undress them before sex, but virtually none who will make you dress them *afterwards*?

Sometimes, one of my cats will do something so sexy in front of me that I want to *slip her a dollar*!

I met this girl who was so cute that it made me want to fuck her with a dick a LOT bigger than mine!

Space-Time Cunt-in-you-um: If you have the space, I have the time! Want to make a universe?

Have you ever had a chick not want to clean herself up after you have fucked her, and she's like, "YOU made the mess; you can go ahead and clean it up!"?

If you are in bed with a very active chick, and she flips around just a little too much, you can accidentally end up tossing it into the wrong basket...

A bird in the hand is worth two fingers in her bush.

This girl was so pretty that when she smiled it made me come a little in my pants; I'm such a dike!

Chapter 5: Simple Weirdness

This chapter contains random, bizarre, and weird thoughts. It is not so much a venture into humor as it is into strangeness.

When people ask me what I think about this cuntry, I tell them that I have a peach orchard that never bears fruit, and a pussy willow that never flowers.

Have you ever farted loudly and woken yourself up?

"The only REAL culture is created by one's own hands, NOT by an assembly line."
- Me 2013

If treason is a requirement for the aristocracy, then paranoia on the part of the slave class is also required.

TV advertisements are like cigarettes: they just *fucking stink*!

God is a total failure.

Have you ever noticed that a baby can fart, and it can be cute? Or that a woman can poot a little one out and it can still be charming? When a man farts, it is never either cute or charming!

I once heard that you need to know the difference between "shit" and "Shinola". The real trick is being able to *turn* shit into Shinola!

Turning human lives into collateral damage is part of the basic skill-set of a billionaire.

"This one's a keeper", you say? This is my woman, and this *scun's* a reaper!

It is not a prerequisite for something to *have* a liver, before it can be delivered?

I am not even a guy; I am just a dude.

Have you ever noticed that the functioning of a woman's body is *exothermic*, while the functioning of her heart is *endothermic*?

I am the spiritual leader of a commune, so I have learned to not trust *hippie types*!

I have heard of racing time, but have you ever heard of *e*rasing it?

It sucks when you are given only the choice between virginity and celibacy!

For some reason, it is a sexual turn-on for a woman to reject me.

I have heard that, "actions speak louder than words". This is certainly true when you action is to discharge a firearm!

I think that there are a lot of guys who want to know what sex is like, but the closest they get is the internet!

If you have the sad misfortune of being born with a dick, there is no way you will die *not* a virgin!

Drink like yer angry!

My favorite thing about a woman is her *pussy*!

I don't have a "yes" to an advertisement. I only have the "no".

Once upon a time, I met a person. It was the worst experience I have ever had.

Being "vegan" automatically makes a person gay.

I have never met chickens who didn't want to play with their shit after you have hauled it out of their shed...

Cuntrary to popular belief, I don't hate people for being gay. I hate them for being *people*.

For a penis, it doesn't have to feel good. It only has to feel GOOD ENOUGH!

Do you have a *predisposition* for being a cunt cyborg?

Even pussy-fucking can be taken too far. I have *seen* the ruins of uncontrolled heterosexuality!

I don't mean to be egotistical, but I have no choice. I am the only person who has sex with me.

Men like to deconstruct women's clothing with their minds. That's why I like skinny chicks. It is easy to see exactly what they would look like naked. Fat women are harder. It's like mentally removing a tent from an elephant!

Why do they call a judge "your honor" when most of them are dishonorable?

I was grounded for the first 9 months of my life, and I hadn't even done anything wrong!

If I eat something salty, I very quickly have the desire to drink something. If I then drink and alcoholic beverage, I almost immediately have the need to urinate. So if I don't want to have to go to the bathroom, it would be better to avoid... salt?

To me, censorship just *feels like* an attack upon the constitution.

Sore losers suck; people who are crappy winners suck a thousand times more.

What is the difference between one of Satan's turds and a Republican?

With God, you can use reverse psychology.

Do hypochondriacs have pantries?

God is a rageaholic!

In order for us ALL to survive, we have to take culture and control of nature back from the aristocracy.

It says, "This bag is not a toy." Try telling that to my cats!

My dog caught and killed a rabbit, then refused to eat it because he found a hare in his food.

I was going through such a fucking lifetime crisis, if I *had* gone through a mid-life crisis at the *same time*, who would have known?

There are not usually a lot of manure hauling related injuries on a farm. What are you going to say? You hauled some manure? Were you hospitalized? Shall I send a sympathy card?

I prefer to chop wood on a sunny day. Cloudy days are too depressing to chop wood.

I DESPISE organized religions, because they are so GOD DAMNED sacrilegious!

I am glad that I haven't died, but I think that I deserve to be younger than THIS right now!

If you are terrified of people, circumnavigation becomes an essential skill.

Wearing clothing makes me want to kill people. I think that is why there are nudist colonies. A lot of people feel how unnatural it is to cover one's body.

Viagra? I have better than that. I have VIANGER!

When you cannibalize a human, the data is more important than the meat.

I sometimes sleep in a box in my living room so that I can feel homeless and yet safe at the same time...

I once knew a demon that drank my soul; she was great sex!

Do you ever drink to see the rate that time passes speed up? They say that time passes faster when you are having fun. The same is true when you are drunk!

I have never met a heterosexual woman.

I was born with a birth defect that makes it nearly impossible to get laid: it's called a penis.

Why is it that the show "60 Minutes" seems to go on for WAY FUCKING LONGER than sixty minutes?

True Story: I once paid a prostitute who proceeded to explain that she was *not* going to have sex with me. Instead, she fed me cold fried chicken and pizza.

When it comes to the basics, there is no difference between a politician and a crack whore.

It should be our motto: "America: What a load of fuckin' crap!"

My face tastes like your ass. I said this to a cat.

Fuck the NEWS! If I want information, I'll make it up myself!

I told my cat, "I like your pussy." She liked the irony.

Some call them Jews or Hebrews. I call them God's Niggas.

In school, I actually *cared* about learning! How passé is that?

Nature is a *CUNT*!

Why would you *want* to have rights anyway? They are kind of passé these days, wouldn't you say?

I sneezed so hard that my asshole felt treated really violently!

Aristocracy plans obsolescence for human beings.

W.C. Field was quoted as saying, "I never met a man I didn't like." I am now fifty years old, and I have *never* met someone who I *do* like!

My wife had little regard for the content of her speech. However, the delivery was important to her; she *always* spoke in anger.

If you buy a manufactured beverage of any kind, or eat American junk food, you are evil, and a traitor to the taxed and unrepresented slave class of the world.

If you own a cell phone, you are a retarded evil traitorous robot. Fuck you in the ass with your cell phone as you suck Satan's cock!

The aristocracy uses junk food as a weapon to destroy your family's bodily health, and the media to destroy their minds.

They like to keep you waiting at a barber shop. In fact, the wait is half of the purpose for being there!

A fly with a mostly barren vagina...?

Why is it that chicks are so cowardly that they are scared of a boner?

She defined herself by the measure of my agony...

All advertisement is a form of psychological attack.

I got so drunk that I *forgot* that I could GET more drunk!

Insurance is insane. I am frequently contacted about a "rape quote". Why would I pay to be raped?
They also often offer me a "Family Rape Plan".
Why would anyone plan to have their family raped?
They offer a "flat rape" too; is that when they lay you on your back to do it?
There is also a "group rape plan"; isn't that known as a "gang bang"?
One thing is certain when it comes to insurance: you are getting *fucked* when you pay the bill!

There are many kinds of intelligence. I suffer from the advantage of being insane.

Have you ever heard of someone doing something just to "pass time"?

What time are they trying to pass? All of it until they are dead?
Do humans just shit time out their entire lives, from birth to death?

Even the Romans knew how to sell the same item for the same price with a lesser quality to a slave, and a higher quality to an aristocrat. The Bush family does the same thing.

Perhaps God *did* create the world in seven days, but it didn't play video games during that period. It didn't have time to "chat" or "message", and it didn't have a cell phone to distract it!

In a couple of generations, humans will be born with the innate ability to kill billionaires.

I heard that the "pen is mightier than the sword"; if so then the media is the pen, and with my sword, I can still chop off their fucking heads!

I can get so drunk that everything I say sounds profound to me!

I don't want to die *now*; it's too early! What time do you have? That is, what time is it?

White people have the innate ability to be "natives" where ever they settle - including Iowa!

Saying: "Humanity has already lost the war, but the revolution never ends until it is victorious!"

America no longer has a system of education; it has a system of disinformation!

Portia wouldn't even blow me off in person; she sent out a friend to do it for her... :(

Advancing technology is one of the greatest dangers to humanity.

Molestation is *not* a form of entertainment to the person *being molested*!

Have you ever heard of "hu-manitee"?

They were "good criminal - bad criminal"-ing this cop...

Did I get drunk today? FUCK NO! I got drunk *yesterday*. Today is simply a matter of *maintaining* the drunk!

Sometimes I do things half-assed; other times I do them half-asked. There are some things that you should *never* do when fully asked!

I was not given life; I was given a *life sentence* and now I am *stuck here* until I am *dead*!

The aristocracy regularly consumes human flesh for nutrition and enjoyment, so society now has a FOOD class of human beings!

If you mess with me, I will fuck you in ways that I am YET TO INVENT!

My libido *alone* is so powerful that it is classified as a *lethal weapon* by the FBI!

I am everything; if you see me in any other way, then I become invisible.

How do you think a carrot feels when it sees a vegan coming?

If you can't *control* people's minds, then there is NO POINT in having a religion!

"The suicide cult of the American obeisaholic"

There's some kind of crap on the floor. No... My mistake; that crap IS the floor!

Does there come a time of day when you hike your panties and skirt up *just a little higher*?

Women are mean. I once had a woman let me fuck with the back of her bra for 30 minutes, before saying, "The snap's in the front."! :-(

There's no point in being innocent if they are going to punish you anyway.

Pussy is a myth. Even starving Ethiopian men beat off wishing that there is pussy on a woman. Overpoopulation? Women can spontaneously make themselves pregnant so that they have kids to punish and yell at.

I saw this guy riding a bike and drinking a Mountain Dew at the same time! The irony was horrible! He might as well have been taking vitamins while sitting in his car with the engine on and the garage doors closed!

"I am sorry President Obama, the insult written in the snow was of your wife's urine, but it was Hillary's handwriting!"

Look at it this way; if China has more *people* than any other cuntry, then they also have the most *pussy*!

Many Asian cultures are now trying to imitate Western culture. But Western culture sucks shit, so these Asian countries are trying their hardest to *suck shit as well*!

Pussies are awesome, but dicks SUCK!

Kate Beckinsale is the "spoonful of sugar that makes the medicine go down"!

I don't have a status in Facebook. In fact, I have no status in life at all!

Do you know what it is like to be inside a womb when you have claustrophobia? It fucking sucks!

How to tell that a person is lying: (by the way this always works) carefully examine the muscles of the face and note the behavior of the muscles around the lips. Now note whether the person is saying something. If they are speaking, they are lying.

If a woman has a cellular phone, I don't consider her a person, and I don't consider her a living thing. Fortunately, I am not opposed to a little necrophilia!

In Iowa, I am surrounded by Homo sapiens bardus. Where I find that my education never ends, I find that most people's never starts!

Cannibalism? Fuck you! Eat me!

Fuck the internet being out! At least I won't get spam email!

Eating junk food is like doing heroine or smoking cigarettes; it should be done in private where no one else has to be exposed to it.

Food for slaves is manufactured by corporations. Free humans grow and raise their own sources of animal and plant based nutrition.

Every day, world-wide, there are billions of women who say "no" to a man. Unless she is a hooker, do you know how many women say yes? None. Women do not sleep with men.

Farmers don't just work with manure. They ARE manure!

Nixon didn't just run a rogue, criminal presidency. That's normal these days. He was just ahead of his time!

The world has changed a lot in the last thousand years or so. Back then, a LOT of women had vaginas...

Wimpling: A very weak, shitty person.

When I wrote that, I was not just on fire, I was on Kindle fire!

ICBM = International Corrupt Billionaire Mobsters

One thing I like about publishing books is that they don't BLOW UP in the FUCKING KILN!

If you are a woman, everyone wants to sleep with you. If you are a man, no one wants to fuck you. Even gay men don't really like to have sex with men; they are just not that into women.

My girlfriend showed up in a *really* cute and short skirt and said, "I'm not wearing any panties!" To which I replied, "Amazing! Neither am I!"

Most people think that the news contains truth. That is why it has been turned into the primary source of lies, propaganda, and brainwashing.

How can someone spew so many lies without even saying anything?

Conversion of mass to energy should have a consistent unit of measure.

The way that the Iraqi people are treated by Americans is as bad as or worse than what we did to the blacks and the Native Americans.

I want to smash in Donald Rumsfeld's face with a baseball bat inscribed with pictures of apple pie and the American flag!

You can bang me in any category, but you can't bang me *into* any category!

Calling a person "old" in a negative way is only attempting to make them feel bad about NOT being dead yet.

The "Mental Discipline of Paranoia": When it comes to humans, if you don't watch your ass, you LOSE it!

For someone to be as STUPID as an Iowan takes *special* training!

Billionaires' lying in the media is "media treason". Like Obama.

"TLC" = "True Loving Care" 4 "The Littlest Cat"

Some people question whether George W. Bush's occupation of Iraq was legal; as far as I am concerned, his occupation of the USA was not legal.

Have you ever heard of a rutabagar? I have never met a polite beggar.

Well, if you are going to be a slut, why fuck around?

I'm just a soul whose dimensions are good; Oh Lord please don't let me be Miss Understood.

One of the most miserable things to do is either get clothes onto or off of a sweaty fat man!

The only thing that "works" for me is being with a woman, and the only thing that works for a woman is being with anyone who is NOT me!

See that cat hair in my frying pan? I actually *plan* to eat it!

According to the Holy Bible, white people have no souls.

I didn't get the mail today. I didn't feel like it. I didn't female like it either.

Humans are so primitive and yet primates are so human...

I like spinning around. You know what they say: "All is right with the whirled."

Gorgeous Woman Brain Lag: When I meet a woman I am strongly attracted to, it takes me about thirty years to know what to say to her. That means that if I met the gal of my dreams today, I will know what to say to her in about 2043, and by then, I will be 80 years old!

The USA is the incarnation of GREED, a deadly sin.

I need a shit. It is a sequence of first a shot, and then a hit.

My wife wasn't just angry, she was furious with a vengeance!

America is a disease, and the primary symptom is obesity.

The massive American red, white, and blue anal probe...

People make a big deal over the abortion issue. What about the fetus' right to choose? I think that they should have some sort of a gladiatorial arena where fetuses could have the opportunity to fight to the death for the right to be born!

The best profession for a child molester is driving an ice cream truck!

My friends came back from a duck-hunting trip, and said that they didn't even get a shot in. I told them, "No harm, no fowl."

The list of people that I trust in this world is short. In fact, I can count it on one hand, but I am going to be *polite* enough to not count it on my RIGHT hand! ;)

The more they put it in the media, the more the lies have an effect.

People are torn out of culture so that they can be put into society.

I finished working on my sewage line yesterday and I am SO GLAD to have that SHIT DONE!

The only "Good" human is a dead one; they are poorly behaved while alive...

Most men know that it is nearly IMPOSSIBLE to get a woman to say "yes" to anything! That is why some guys are necrophiliacs; the "yes" is automatic!

Since I am alone on my commune, I have very little "comm"; it's mostly just the "une".

My friend said that in a world-wide disaster emergency, he doesn't want to eat his kids. I told him, "Oh come on! They are DELICIOUS if they are prepared right!"

If society can't give itself love and kindness, it can't give it to you either.

Politics have made themselves obsolete; if they have no actual power to help humanity, then they have no power at all.

The saddest thing about modern day Chinese and Indian culture is that they wanted to badly to be like the USA that they ACUTALLY MANAGED TO DO IT!

The poorer you are, the more likely you are to GET YOUR FUCK ON!

I kiss posters of pretty women because they don't turn away from me.

If she wants to be a cunt, she is *going* to be a cunt. I can't "un-cunt" her...

I wake up every morning with some pussy hairs encrusted around my mouth.

I wouldn't be so tired if I were not so totally exhausted!

Isn't the act of having humans as children passé anyway?

If even GOD can't get you laid, then you're not going to GET laid!

Foxes are not actually very closely related to dogs and wolves. They have a genius of their own.

A man can get a hard-on. Can he get a fart-on?

American shopping carts cause cancer. Literally.

They say that I "wear my heart on my sleeve". That's so I can leave it with my shirt in my locker, and be heartless when I go out to play.

There was ONE TIME in recorded history when a woman willingly had sex with a man. I think it was the 80's. I'm not sure which century...

It used to be illegal to teach a slave to read or write. It isn't anymore. You just don't want to teach them TOO MUCH!

If you enter into a marriage with a vagina, you had better be prepared to have sex at any given moment 24/7 for the rest of your life.

"When I am kissing a girl, and her breasts are pressing up against my throat, I think its special..." Well, I am crazy, so it is not very surprising that I could come up with this thought; as far as I can tell, it is at least sincere.

If someone is both a Hebrew and a Jew, you can call it a "Brew". The same is true if a Hebrew marries a Jew. Their child is called a "Brew".

Dinosaurs are NOT smart. They just have the power to hire those who are.

For some reason, stupid people have an evolutionary advantage over smart people. This seems logically contradictory. Look at George W. Bush. He is completely retarded, yet extremely rich. At some point, his stupidity became and advantage.

Chapter 6: Random Stuff

Tongue Twister: She sells; she sells, down there where she's sore!

Quote: "A billionaire is more destructive than a nuclear weapon." - Curtis Crim 2013

Varying levels of trouser defecation: A baby "poops" his diapers, but a 50 year old "Craps" his pants!

A Poem "The Consumer"
 By Curtis Crim:
"Ours is just to watch you die,
 Ours is just to stand on by,
 Ours is not to reason why,
 Ours is just to *spend* and *buy*!"

Song: "I'm reaming up a white asshole"
I'm reaming up a white asshole, with every asshole card I wipe!
May your gays be Mary and Sioux,
And may all the assholes be you!

Country Song: (To be sung in a heavy, rural, country drawl)

"Why have a heart if it's gonna' be broken?
Why have a heart if it's gonna' be sad?
Why have a heart, when you know your part -
Is to be heart-broken, and sad!

I'm gonna' donate my heart to science!

Please don't wait until I am dead;
I can't stand my heart, because I know I part,
Is to be heart-broken, and sad.

Tell doc he don't have to scrub first;
Not much more harm that he can do.
They can sell the part, that is called my heart;
It's just too heart-broken, and sad.

You can even get the butcher to do it.
He won't have to even slice it up.
It will fall apart, 'cause you know my heart,
Is so heart-broken, and sad!

Don't try to glue it back together.
No way to repair the harm was done...
As sure as I fart, you know that my poor heart,
Will always be heart-broken, and sad!"

My Vaunted Sibling

Have you met my sister? Now, she is a healer, but
as a teen she was a squealer!

If my sister the "healer" were to die of cancer, the
irony alone would fucking kill me!

I could fertilize my *WHOLE FARM* with the
amount of shit that my sister dumps on my head!

You pushed that THING out of your vagina? Why
didn't you just give birth to Satan like my mother
did?

My sister never lost her taste for being molested...

My sister wrote a mostly autobiographical musical and titled it, "Okla-hooooooooooo-bag!"

If you are failing to treat my sister like a whore, then you are simply failing!

Anyone who can give me $2 a pound can fuck my sister! That's a reasonable price for organic produce, isn't it?

I have never met ANYONE who fucked my sister and DIDN'T take her for a whore!

Aching Breaking Fart

Don't smell my fart, my Aching Breaking Fart!
You'll find I'm a very stinky man.

And if you smell my fart, my aching breaking fart,
It might be something you can't stand!

Don't smell my fart, my aching breaking fart!
An act I couldn't understand...

And if you smell my fart, my aching breaking fart,
You'll find yourself another man!

Chapter 7: Fun with Sound

The contents of this chapter all contain some sort of phonetic, or sound-based, element(s).

Terrible, treasonous terrorists tend to own territory in Texas.

Did you say "cannibalistic" or "cannon ballistic"?

"Am I the one who brews the wine?" How the fuck does one *bruise* wine?

"Attacks right off" or "a tax write off"?

Did you say "scissors and bag", or "my sister's a hag"?

Continue? Or there's a cunt in you?

What is the difference between a bee feeder and a beef eater?

Did you say that you need to read on the way?
No; I said that I have weed on the tray!

Did you say "egg hunt" or "a cunt"? If you are a guy who wants children, then they both *come* down to the same thing, really.

If you had to bear a cross, would you bear a cross across a bridge?

A folk song from New Guinea: "Thank Heaven for little girls! Without them what would little boys stew?"

Is it men's "crew" socks, or men "screw socks"?

Chapter 8: Bits, Trips, & Rants

Iowan etiquette on stealing is really strange. If someone takes something of yours without asking in front of you, then you "gave" it to them.

When I was a teenager, none of the chicks would make out with me because I was creepy and horrible. Now I am also 50.

I have actually had gals tell me, "I can't sleep with you because you are on the rebound." :(

How can some people get addicted to sex when others can't even get laid in six years?

You should not be defined by what you put into your shopping cart. Or should you?

Trip: I used to date this chick who was in a coma. I broke up with her when I caught her in bed with another man (I think he was the janitor in her ward). I was SO pissed off at her; the bitch got pregnant with her new boyfriend! Then her Dad found out, and was furious. I don't think it was because she got pregnant so much as he just didn't want her to have a baby with a Mexican!

DNA evolves almost as quickly as human technology... This is very dangerous!

I have heard that out of the billions of people on the planet, conservatively millions are having sex this very moment. That's just *normal* sex. How many sheep and goats are getting raped as you read this text? Do you seriously think that there are not at least thousands of children who have a penis going in and out of their bodies this very moment? Now, how many men at this very second are fucking a corpse?

On the "Immaculate Conception of Jesus Christ: Even if it *was* an immaculate conception, which just means that God fucked another man's wife - WHICH IS *ADULTERY*! That isn't right even if you are God. It also means that Jesus was born out of wedlock, so he is God's bastard. Mary was not willing, so it was an act of rape. Mary was also thirteen years old at the time, so it was an act of pedophilia. Last, we are all God's children so this was an act of *incest* on the part of God! The impregnation of Mary, mother of Jesus, was one of the most evil acts ever performed in the universe!

What if people could get high on catnip? Would it be regulated, and would kitties have to buy it from a "back alley cat"?
Would they then go down to the Pink Pussy Cafe and order some Amsterdam hashish, and watch cute little kitties dance around naked?

When I was a kid, my parents never gave me any pussy. Neither did my sister. In fact, none of my relatives ever gave me any pussy. For my birthday, I never got any pussy. In high school and college, I never got any pussy. I have a CAT, and HE never gives me any pussy! I don't know what the FUCK is wrong with chicks, but none of them give me any pussy. I go to the store, and can't locate the pussy. The bank, again no pussy. I really am at a loss. I am

50 now, and have never been able to find it.
WHERE THE FUCK DO YOU FIND PUSSY?
Amazon? I sure as FUCK didn't find any on eBay!

Watching a vegetarian hunt vegetables is a brutal
experience. The vegetable is frequently ripped from
the ground, tearing at its roots while it is still alive
and conscious.
Plants are forced together in uncomfortable
conditions for the purpose of mass production. The
feelings of these plants are usually entirely
disregarded. They are not spoken to appreciatively
as their fruits are torn or cut from their bodies. They
are forced to live in unnatural conditions in order to
exploit them for vegetable nutrition.
Many of these vegetables are also eaten while still
living, without the decency of even being killed or
cooked first. Some vegetarians eat the seeds and
nuts of plants, harming future generations. Many
other vegetables are put on cutting boards, and
viciously sliced to pieces while still conscious! The
fact is, humans are brutal to not only animals, but
also plants and other humans (such as billionaires
raising and eating human meat taken from the slave
class.) Simply put, if you are going to live,
something must be exploited, killed, and consumed.
I strongly suggest that one at least eat food that is
home grown, prepared and home, and home cooked.

Short Story idea: A billionaire takes a commercial
space flight. He is provided a satellite imaging
interface that allows him to select a specific young
girl in a third-world country.
He places his order with the kitchen and within
minutes the girl is kidnapped and delivered to the

space station, butchered, and prepared with a cordon blue sauce and served to the aristocrat.

There comes a point in life when reality becomes entirely elective. My Mother once commented, "There are way too many Jews on the moon." This left me confused. There is little point in trying to contradict a statement like that, so I decided to go along with it. I told her, "That's because the Moon is now the Earth's most modern vacation resort/concentration camp."

"Nature needs a reboot" I'm just saying…

I have never been anything like a human. I have never been accepted by humans. I have far more powers than a human. I have come to the conclusion that I must be a demi-god. I do not have the power to create a universe like various Gods (Natalie Portman, for one). Nor am I so helpless that I cannot create a universe at all. I just take the known universe, and filter out what I don't find useful in creation, and the results are seen on my organic farm. As a demigod, I have powers like a super hero, but most people cannot see them just by looking at me. I will now tell you about my super hero powers!

When it comes to women, I have the power of:

  - Invisibility: - If I don't hit on a woman, she *literally* cannot see me at all. No woman ever talks to me or starts a conversation with me. In a grocery store, they can run into me physically, look quite confused, and not know what they ran into, and can't see a person in front of them. They see nothing. I am invisible to women *all of the time!*

- Psychic-ness: - I am psychic. I have the power of mental telepathy. I don't even know why this works so well, but women *always* know what I am thinking! That's right. Whenever I am talking with a woman whom I either don't know or hardly know (and honestly, I don't know anyone), somewhere in my mind, I have the desire to insert my penis into her vagina, and they *always* seem to know it. I don't understand how this is possible, but it works *every time!*

- Increased movement speed: - Have you ever heard of Quicksilver (Marvel) or The Flash (DC Comics)? I somehow can make a woman move faster just by being in her general vicinity. This is a way for a man to know whether a woman is interested in him or not. If you attempt to start a conversation with a woman whom you find interesting, try to put some attention on whether she starts moving away from you at an increased rate. You might have not touched a woman in years, and you might be *very* interested in getting to know her, so you might try to keep up with her while trying to keep up some simple conversation. Perhaps she starts pushing her cart even faster, so you try to move onto something more impressive, and increase your movement speed as well. For some reason, women always move faster and faster until I see them transition from a trot to a gallop. That is when I realize that my super power is giving them increased movement speed, and I let her go on with her shopping.

- Repelling: - I am not sure about how this works, or the physics involved in the phenomenon. For some reason, the closer I am to a woman geographically, the faster she moves away from me proportionately. No matter how hard I try to get within the distance to even have a conversation, a woman always moves away from me at my pace increased exponentially. The woman doesn't even usually know that this is caused by my super hero power.

- Super human speed: - I have actually seen this happen on more than one occasion. If I kiss a woman, she then has the ability to move away from me at speeds that one would normally think impossible. Tires burn. The rubber souls of shoes melt. Materials ignite. One girl named Ginny nearly ran me over after I kissed her intimately. She nearly knocked me over diving away in her Ford Falcon, and I think you can still see the skid marks on the street in front of 336 Garfield, in Ft. Collins, CO. And that was over 20 years ago!

- Quantum shift: I do not live in a universe where a woman can show me the smallest amount of attention. Somehow, that doesn't happen in the *quantum* version of my universe that I seem to exist within. I truly believe that if I were to sit even for a few seconds with a charming, intelligent, and alluring woman that such energies would be released as to cause a shift in quantum realities! I would *literally* land in a different version of this universe!

"Cunnilingual bilabial aero-phonic technique":
is pretty simple. If you have played the trombone or

any instrument in the trumpet family, you already know how to perform a vibrating embouchure. One good warm-up is to buzz into your mouthpiece without the horn attached. You can put your hands over the horn end to simulate the pressure resistance you would normally have if the mouthpiece was attached to the horn. Now, you can also warm up your embouchure without the mouthpiece. Practice "buzzing" your embouchure with no instrument at all. Play scales and basic techniques. Play simple tunes that you know. When your embouchure is warm, play "happy birthday" as you press your lips against your girlfriend's clitoris. You can also use your vocal chords as you whistle against her clit. This is called the, "sing and whistle" by some people. I call it "whirring".

The objective is to make various vibrations with your lips and mouth in such a way that causes your gal screaming orgasms! Curious, it is impossible to get a woman to say "yes" to a date, so even if you are good at it, you will probably never get a chance to use these techniques.

Billionaires are Terrorists and Traitors: So, a few people with no morals at all got super rich selling fossil fuels. After the illegal takeover of all the governments on the planet Earth (in the year 2000), they then decided to charge money for air. The more "air" they put in a box or bottle, the more they can then hike up the price of that item. You can now pay $10 for a bottle that only has 1 oz of water, and is mostly filled with air. Both should be free.

Then they decided to tax rain. If rain falls on your property, you can get good produce growth, so it seemed reasonable to tax it. Then, Iowa got terrible flooding rains. Farmers were losing entire crops. Mortgages were not getting paid. Billionaires came in and told people who had already lost EVERYTHING that they owed taxes that were beyond reason. The aristocracy decided that the debt *could* be paid using human resources. Farmers are now being incarcerated and sold into slavery to pay the debt that was generated by the natural phenomenon that destroyed their homes and crops. Entire families are being broken up for the profit of monsters. No billionaire has ever made a positive contribution to society. They are all monsters.

"I have a sinus in my shoulder!" I don't even know what this fucking means. All I can conclude is that I must have been *really* fucked up when I thought to write it down!

If you have the munchies, you should have to look no farther than you shelves. If you have to go as far as the fridge, then you are far too desperate! ← Yep. Pretty much drunk when this one came out too.

It has recently come to the attention of lawmakers that Iowa has no system of education. It's not like the retards don't try; it's just that they don't have anyone who has enough intelligence to teach another human. They tried testing students with essays, but found that they can neither write nor read the essay questions. They tried multiple choice, but found that students with *no* education can't answer the questions correctly. Then they tried True or False questions, but found that these students with no education somehow managed to get the answer wrong 100% of the time, when statistically they should have hit at about 50% just by *chance and guessing*. So, they came up with a new kind of examination question: it is called the "Single choice question". They ask a question and supply only ONE answer, and it is always correct if selected. This baffled Iowan students more than ever. They now only need to choose the ONLY answer provided, and they still manage to *not choose anything* and get the answer wrong over *ninety percent of the time*! Here is an actual example: I needed to have my propane tank refilled, but Access Energy was taken over by traitors who stole the accounts and contracts of slaves who have no choice in the matter. The guy who drives the refill truck made it to the top of the driveway, got confused, and went back to the main office. They called me and told me that their delivery man just couldn't figure out which driveway to go down. Here's the catch: there is only ONE driveway. I am on the South side of the road, and it is *miles* in either direction to get to any other driveway. It's not like he could have been confused because he had SO MANY options to choose from. There is only *one* driveway, and either you drive down it or you don't. There was only ONE answer, the correct one, and this guy came by *three times* and couldn't figure out which one out of *one* was the right one to go down. THERE IS NOWHERE FUCKING ELSE TO GO and yet the bastard kept going back to the main office insisting that out of *one* possibility, he just was not able to choose the right one! That's right: out of ONE option, he could not figure out which one is the right one! HOW FUCKING STUPID CAN YOU GET? Well, you can be Iowan. That's pretty fucking *stupid!*

And the Winner Is:

They say that God created the universe in seven days. It was actually five days, and she was *bleeding the WHOLE TIME!*